TRACTION

QUADRUPLE YOUR BUSINESS IMMEDIATELY WITH THESE MARKETING TECHNIQUES

Jonathan S. Walker

Copyright © 2017 Jonathan S. Walker

All rights reserved.

DEDICATION

This Book Is Dedicated To All Who Desire To Be Financially Free. May Your Efforts Bear Fruits In the Near Future And I Wish You All The Success In Life.

&

I dedicate this book as well to my two beautiful children and my loving wife who have been nothing short of being my light and joy throughout the years.

Copyright 2017 by Jonathan S. Walker - All rights reserved.

The following eBook is reproduced below with the goal of providing information that is as accurate and reliable as possible. Regardless, purchasing this eBook can be seen as consent to the fact that both the publisher and the author of this book are in no way experts on the topics discussed within and that any recommendations or suggestions that are made herein are for entertainment purposes only. Professionals should be consulted as needed prior to undertaking any of the action endorsed herein.

This declaration is deemed fair and valid by both the American Bar Association and the Committee of Publishers Association and is legally binding throughout the United States.

Furthermore, the transmission, duplication or reproduction of any of the following work including specific information will be considered an illegal act irrespective of if it is done electronically or in print. This extends to creating a secondary or tertiary copy of the work or a recorded copy and is only allowed with express written consent from the Publisher. All additional right reserved.

The information in the following pages is broadly considered to be a truthful and accurate account of facts and as such any inattention, use or misuse of the information in question by the reader will render any resulting actions solely under their purview. There are no scenarios in which the publisher or the original author of this work can be in any fashion deemed liable for any hardship or damages that may befall them after undertaking information described herein.

Additionally, the information in the following pages is intended only for informational purposes and should thus be thought of as universal. As befitting its nature, it is presented without assurance regarding its prolonged validity or interim quality. Trademarks that are mentioned are done without written consent and can in no way be considered an endorsement from the trademark holder.

CONTENTS

Part 1

Introduction

Chapter 1: Do You Have Traction?

Chapter 2: Offline

Chapter 3: Emails

Chapter 4: Viral

Chapter 5: Public Speaking

Part 2

Chapter 1: Social Media Marketing And its Impact in 2015

Chapter 2: Social Media Case Studies

Chapter 3: Social Media Accounts – What's Best For Your Business

Chapter 4: Doing Social Media Marketing The Right Way

Conclusion

VIP Subscriber List

Dear Reader, If you would like to receive latest tips and tricks on internet marketing, exclusive strategies, upcoming books & promotions, and more, do subscribe to my mailing list in the link below! I will be giving away a free book that you can download right away as well after you subscribe to show my appreciation!

Here's the link: http://bit.do/jonathanswalker

INTRODUCTION

Congratulations on purchasing your personal copy of *Traction*. Thank you for doing so.

The following chapters will discuss some of the many ways that you can build your businesses traction.

You will discover the importance of marketing and the effect that it can have on your business and its success.

There are plenty of books on this subject on the market, thanks again for choosing this one! Every effort was made to ensure it is full of as much useful information as possible. Please enjoy!

Congratulations on downloading your personal copy of *Traction*. Thank you for doing so.

DO YOU HAVE TRACTION?

New startup companies and businesses will often have a hard time getting up and running. Being able to get the capital to fund a new business and keep it going can be hard for new businesses that don't have the time to prove their abilities in the marketplace. When a business creates traction, it helps the company to attract possible investors and gain an edge over their competition.

Business traction tells us the progress a new business has and its momentum it gains as it grows. There isn't a certain way that a company can measure traction, but most businesses rely on their revenue and how customers respond to their product. The reason for traction is to make sure the business grows and meets certain objectives and goals. This may seem like an abstract thought, it is imperative and allows a business to understand where, in the industry, it stands and where they want to get.

Traction may be important to the company's founders

and workers; it is also equally important to stakeholders and investors who are interested in the organization. The better the traction, the more investors that company will attract. As a result of attracting more investors, the company will also have more funds available to them to help them succeed. This means that developing good business traction is imperative to all new businesses and should be a part of the company's business plan.

The first steps to creating a successful startup are, understanding the organization's future, creating goals, and figuring out a way to reach those goals. Having clearly stated goals in your mission statement and your business plan will show investors how they can expect the company to progress in relation to the factors of the marketplace and competition. However, just coming up with your goals isn't enough. To know your traction, you have to understand the metrics you will be using to define your success. Depending on what industry you're in and the external factors of the marketplace, traction could be measured through market research, sales, or customer response.

Even the most well-intentioned company, with a perfect business plan, can still struggle to find traction. There are millions of reasons as to why so many startups fail, the most common is a lack of brand or product awareness. When competition begins to grow in the marketplace, the smaller businesses that aren't as well known will become overwhelmed by larger brands. To avoid this problem, new companies need to increase the marketing and advertising efforts.

OFFLINE

When online marketing started to grow in popularity, people forgot about the many proven offline marketing methods. Online marketing is important, many of the other techniques in this book are online, but engaging your customer's offline is a distinct and unique method that shouldn't be forgotten.

If you're looking to boost your marketing, start trying some outside of the box tactics. Let's look at five almost forgotten offline marketing methods that require little to no budget.

OFFLINE GUERRILLA MARKETING

Guerrilla marketing refers to the use of unique marketing methods, and since online marketing is so strictly structured, offline is the easiest area to try out some guerrilla marketing tactics. At this point, you can forget everything you know about how marketing channels work and allow your inner child to have some fun. Offline guerrilla methods include:

- Create temporary images on cars, buildings, etc. with sticky notes.

- Create branded bookmarks and give them to your local library.

- "Accidentally" leave behind a pen with your brand on it at the bank.

- Draw advertisements on the sidewalk with chalk.

- Place sticky notes with your business on it in random places.

BUSINESS CARDS

This is a guerrilla tactic that needs to be talked about specifically. This is a necessity and not an option like the other methods I mentioned earlier. If you run a business of any kind, whether established, small, or a startup, you have to have business cards, and you need to hand them out. Don't just give them to people that you meet; drop them everywhere you go.

Places you should leave behind a business card at:

- Always drop your business card in a contest fish bowl that is asking for cards.
- Place your business cards in books at the library that relates to your company.
- Whenever you see a public bulletin board; pin your business card to it.
- When you pay your bill at a restaurant, leave behind a business card.

PHOTOGRAPH AND FILM EVERYTHING

Since social media marketing is only online, most marketers and owners will forget that they can boost the social campaigns through offline efforts. Simple ways to do so is by taking photos of daily activities and company events and post them online. You can do the same with videos as well. If you or somebody else from your company speaks at an important event, record the speech and upload it to your social media accounts. When you use real-life photos and videos from your company's offline world, you are showing your company's personality and increasing your user engagement. A Facebook post that has a photo will receive 84% more clicks, and two times as many like than a text-only post. There are also a lot of social media networks that are the only image based, such as Tumblr, Pinterest, and Instagram.

DONATE PRODUCTS AND GIFT CERTIFICATES AS A PRIZE

When you offer your service or product as a prize for a local contest, you will build your business's visibility, while also showing that you are committed to your local community. If your business is a beauty supply store, you could donate a gift certificate or a gift basket for your most popular products. The organization you donate the product or service to may even announce your brand prize to a room of sponsors. They may even publish you business names in ads in various publications, like a press release, website, or newsletter.

MAKE PUBLIC APPEARANCES

Public events provide you a great way to build your brand's awareness, meet new people, and share ideas. They become even more effective when you speak at these events. Locate a local event that is related to your industry, figure out what people want to learn about your business, and volunteer to speak. If you don't have the clout to get to speak at these sorts of events, just attending them can be as worthwhile.

You don't have to use all of these offline marketing methods, just start implementing at least one. Write down a promotion on a few sticky notes and take them with you. You never know what could happen.

E-MAILS

Your average consumer's inbox is full of marketing messages with attention-grabbing subject lines trying to compete with you. Each day there are over 144 billion emails sent out; making email marketing one of the best online channels for business marketing and communication. The trick is to separate yourself from everybody else.

Figuring out your key message is important to your bottom line no matter what your goal is. The following eight email strategies will ensure that your emails will stand out amongst your competitions, and will help you achieve your goals.

PERSONALIZE WITHOUT THE CONSUMER'S NAME

You know longer have to worry about "Dear [insert name here]." Having a personalized email greeting isn't as effective as you may think. Research performed by Temple's Fox School of Business has even suggested that this personalization can be harmful. People become wary about emails with personalizing greetings because of the concerns about credit card fraud, phishing, and identity theft.

An important part of email marketing is the relationship. Does your recipient trust you? Does the recipient actually know who you are? When you send out an email the jumps the familiarity gun too soon, your personalization will appear to be a bit sketchy. Intimacy had to be earned in the real world, so emails work the same way.

When you fake familiarity, you will likely turn many of your email readers off. Now, this doesn't mean that all personalization forms are off limits. In fact, certain brand personalizations can help you out: sending an email that gives your subscriber individuality. This could simply mean their purchase history.

This means if you want to personalize your emails, do it in a meaningful way. It doesn't take much of relationship or knowledge to put your consumer's name in your email greeting. Sending a personalized email that is recipient specific shows a lot more care.

THE IMPORTANCE OF SUBJECT LINES

It seems that when it comes down to crafting your subject line, there is only one thing you have to avoid: a 60 to 70 character subject line. Marketers call this the subject length "dead zone." Research performed by Adestra tracked over 900 million emails, and there wasn't any increase in click-through or open rates at the 60 to 70 character subject line length.

On the opposite side of things, subject lines that contained more than 70 characters were more beneficial in engaging readers and getting them to click through to the content and subject lines that at less than 49 characters tested better for email open rates. Surprisingly, they found that subject lines that had less than ten characters at 58% open rate.

The use of short subjects came into vogue when President Barack Obama used them in his fundraising emails. There was amazing engagement with subject lines such as "Wow" and "Hey."

Now the question is: Are you looking for opens or boost

clicks? Create long subject lines for more click-through, or keep them short for more opens. Either way, just make sure that you keep your subject lines out of the 60 to 70 character range.

EMAIL PRIMETIME: 8 PM TO MIDNIGHT

While quality emails may be created during regular business hours, the ones that are more likely to be open aren't sent between nine and five. The best time to send an email is at night. Experian Marketing Services discovered that the emails that received the best open rate had been sent between 8 pm and midnight. This time not only did well for open rates, but it did better for sales and click-through. 8 pm to midnight is also the least used, which helps the late night emails perform better than the rest.

Deployment time and inbox crowding also work together. This means that if your email goes out at a time when others don't, it stands a better chance of being noticed. Mailing your customers at their optimal time will be up to you. You will need to make sure at run some tests to see when you receive the best response.

EVERYBODY LIKES SOMETHING FOR FREE

Consumers love receiving things for free. Bluewire Media tested different types of content on their 6,300 subscribers to find out what free items got the highest clicks and open. Their winners were tools and templates.

Most consumers will want to know what's in it for them and Bluewire Media found that tools and templates greatly outweighed photo albums, brain teasers, expert interviews, and ebooks. You will have to do your own tests with your own subscribers, but using this information is a great head start.

OPENS ON MOBILE DEVICES ACCOUNTED FOR 47% OF ALL OPENS

Look at it this way, if your emails get you $100,000 in sales every month, would you want to say goodbye to $44,000 just because you emails show up weird on mobile devices?

You need to make sure you design you email responsively so that they look great no matter where they are being read. These are some mobile design tips that can help:

- Ergonomic: Most people with scroll and tap with their thumb, so place interactive elements in the middle.

- Make an obvious, and easy to use, call-to-action. Above the fold it best.

- Make sure you follow the iOS guidelines for buttons: 44 pixels wide by 44 pixels tall.

- Make your font size better to make them easier to read on smartphones.

- Change your email to a one column template.

EMAIL IS BETTER THAN TWITTER AND FACEBOOK

Social media may be on email's heels, but the inbox kind still has a greater influence over social media. SocialTwist monitored 119 referral campaigns for over 18 months that were performed by leading companies and brands. They found that there was a significant advantage to an email's ability to create new customers as compared to Twitter and Facebook. There were 300,000 referrals that became new customers, and of that 50.8 % were reached by email, 22 % through Facebook, and 26.8% through Twitter.

EMAIL ON WEEKENDS

Saturday and Sunday didn't outperform the 8 pm to midnight time, but they did outperform the other weekdays. Just like at the 8 to midnight time, a number of emails sent on the weekends are low, which helps your messages to stand out. The margins for sales rates, click-through, and opens were not that substantial, but every little bit counts when it comes to email marketing.

RE-ENGAGING OLD SUBSCRIBERS

You have a huge list, awesome. The problem is that 2/3s of those people are likely inactive. Research has discovered that a subscribers list of inactivity is 63%. This means that once a person joins your list, they are less likely to actually follow up with any of your emails. Listrak has said that the first 90 days are important to change a sign-up to a devotee.

That 63% now needs to be re-engaged. The trick is to figure out what kind of re-engagement campaign will work the best for you followers. It's quite likely, that if you have already been doing research, you have found different kinds of results.

VIRAL

It's true; the term viral marketing does sound offensive. Saying that you are a viral marketer will likely cause people to take a couple of steps back. A virus is a feared thing, which is not quite dead and not completely alive. But you have to admit a virus is admirable. It is able to live in secrecy until it is able to reproduce several times. It even piggybacks onto other hosts to increase its own tribe.

So how does a virus translate to marketing? Viral marketing is a strategy that gets a consumer to pass on a message to other people, which create a potentially exponential growth in the influence and exposure to the message. Like a virus, these strategies take advantage of fast multiplication to send out a message to thousands or even millions.

Hotmail.com is a classic example of viral marketing at work. Their strategy was simple:

1. Give people free email addresses and services

2. They placed a tag at the bottom of each message that said: "Get your private, free email at www.hotmail.com."

3. Then they sat back and waited while people emailed their family and friends

4. People notice the emails

5. Those people register so that they get their own email; all leading up to

6. They pass the word on to a growing number of associates and friends.

Their message spread like the small waves that ripple off of the water after a pebble is dropped into a pond. You too can make a viral marketing strategy that ripples out to more and more people.

Before you begin coming up with your strategy you have to accept the fact that some strategies will work better than other ones depending on your audience. There is very few that work as well as the Hotmail message. But we are going to look at six unique concepts that you should try to use in your marketing plans. Your strategy doesn't have to contain every single one of these elements, but the more that you use, the more powerful your result will become. An effective strategy should try to have:

1. Service or product giveaway
2. Makes it easy to transfer to others
3. Is able to be scaled from small to large
4. Taps into common behaviors and motivations
5. Makes use of existing networks for communication
6. Use others' resources

Let's look at each of these a little more.

SERVICE OR PRODUCT GIVEAWAY

Free, like we've talked about before, is a powerful word in marketing. Most of the viral marketing programs out there will give away valuable services and products to attract their consumer's attention. These free things could be free "cool" buttons, free information, free email services, or free software programs that are able to do powerful things, but not everything that the "pro" version is able to do. The words inexpensive and cheap will generate some interest, but the word free will do the same only faster. Viral marketers aren't afraid of delayed gratification. They are okay with not make any profit today, but if they are able to create a bunch of interest from free things, they will be able to profit soon and for forever. You have to have patience. Free will attract eyeballs, those eyeballs will then wander to the countless things that *aren't* free which you're selling, and there you have sales. Eyeballs will provide you with sales opportunities, email addresses, and advertising revenue.

MAKES IT EASY TO TRANSFER TO OTHERS

Doctors and nurses will tell you that during flu season, you should do everything in your power to avoid being contaminated. This is because viruses are only able to spread when they can be easily transmitted. The medium that you use to carry your marketing message needs to be easily transferred and replicated: software download, graphic, website, and email. Viral marketing works amazingly on the internet since there are inexpensive and easy communication sources. Digital formats make it easy to copy things. When you look at it in terms of marketing, the entire idea is to make things as simple and shareable as possible. Generally, when it comes to a marketing message, short is the way to go. Make sure that your message is copied, compelling, and compressed at the bottom of each of your email messages.

IS ABLE TO BE SCALED FROM SMALL TO LARGE

However you decide to transmit your message, the ultimate goal should be that it's super simple for it to catch fire and spread. To look back at the free email accounts method, there's a fundamental flaw: if the campaign is *too* effective, more users may end up trying to join than server space is available. Otherwise, the new users will be left unaccommodated, and as a result, the campaign will start to fail. Nobody wants a worthless email account, even if it is free. Taking it back to the virus analogy, if the virus is to kill the person that is hosting it before the virus is able to transmit itself, the virus effectively is failing at its job. However, if the email provider were to plan ahead so that the new accounts could certainly be properly be accommodated, regardless of how successful the campaign is, then everything will be alright. The key point is that everything has to be scalable in terms of your campaign; if it can't go from small to big with no problems, then there's a fundamental flaw.

TAPS INTO COMMON BEHAVIORS AND MOTIVATIONS

A good marketing campaign will always tap into humanity's seedy mental underbelly. Greed drives people. People want desperately to be "cool", as well as loved and understood. By taking advantage of these perfectly human tendencies, you'll generate hundreds of thousands of website hits and millions of email mentions. So, in order to build a strong marketing plan, you have to take advantage of our most human qualities and desires; that, friend, is how you build a winning marketing plan.

MAKES US OF EXISTING NETWORKS FOR COMMUNICATION

Most everyone is social. Social scientists have figured out that everybody has at least 12 people in their network of associates, family, and friends. Their broader network might consist of thousands of people; ultimately this depends upon what they do and how important they are. For example, a waiter may talk with a huge number of customers every week. The best marketers are those who have a strong understanding of how powerful these interpersonal bridges can be, whether they are strong interpersonal bridges – like those with family and friends – or weak ones, like with customers. Everybody who uses the internet also has a rather extensive network, as well. They get favorite websites and email addresses. Affiliate marketing programs take advantage of these internet-based networks. The way to rapidly make your message spread is to find your way into these interpersonal connections.

USE OTHERS' RESOURCES

The best marketing strategies are those that take advantage of others' resources to help get the word out. Affiliate marketing plans, for example, put graphic links or text on other people's websites. A single news article, if pertinent and popular, will be taken up by a huge number of other websites and sources of content. Somebody else's web page or newsprint is relying on your marketing message. Somebody else's resources get depleted and not yours.

PUBLIC SPEAKING

One of the many responsibilities of being a small business owner is being the face of your company. You are already the main customer relationship manager. You must be its lead promoter and champion to grow your business. One way that this can be done is to actively participate and attend conferences that are related to your industry. Another way is to give talks to potential customers.

The following resources and tips can help you find speaking opportunities and conferences that are relevant to your business. They can also help you get speaking engagements, too.

Learning to listen before you speak is an excellent idea. Before you begin doing your own presentations you need to attend sessions that others in your fields are giving. You will pick up on what presentations are popular. You might see gaps that you might be able to fill with your own expertise. If you ask questions and provide different insights during the question and answer time during these presentations, you might be remembered if you apply to speak at a related event at a later date.

When you feel like you are ready to represent your business and share your expertise, you will need to find speaking engagements. You need to find groups that are looking for speakers and sell yourself on your talk. The first thing to do is to make a speaker's one-sheet. This is a one-page introduction to your topic and yourself. It will provide a jumping-off point for self-promoting yourself as a speaker.

Now you need to look for organizations that are looking for speakers for certain events. You can do a google search to look for speaking events in your area. There are also paid services that will match speakers with certain event organizers. You can offer your services to groups that may benefit from your expertise.

To be a successful speaker you have to provide some value to your audience. This means that you have to share your expertise not just promote your business. Your first presentation will be the hardest. You will get better with time. You will start getting reviews and testimonials that you will be able to use to help promote yourself as a speaker. You will soon find yourself being regarded as an expert and the face of your company and industry.

Here are some ways to get speaking engagements to help market your business:

1. Become a better speaker: This sounds obvious, but by being a more polished, engaging speaker, you will gain more opportunities to speak. If you are a very good speaker, you can ask for testimonials from the people that invited you to speak. These testimonials go a long way when others are looking for speakers.

   How can you become a better speaker? The best and easiest way is to record each presentation and watch it later. Take notes of what you would like to improve on. Try focusing on different things every time you speak. How you stand, where you put your hands, how you modulate your voice. With time, you will be an extraordinary speaker.

2. Know your material: Knowing your material inside and out will help you become a better speaker because it will ease your nerves. First, you absolutely must know your speech. You need to practice it over and over. By knowing your speech means you can be confident and at ease when you step on a stage and face the crowd. Being prepared is a great way to overcome nerves.

Knowing your speech isn't enough. You must be an expert in your area. The more that you know, the more confident you will be when taking questions from your audience.

The most important thing about your presentation it that it is not a pitch. You should not be trying to sell anything. Give the audience things they can take with them that they can use and actions they can follow. Your main goal is to help them.

3. Have a speaking page on your website: Add a page that promotes yourself as a speaker. It is the best way to get engagements. On this speaking page, post a demo reel, maybe a few clips from a previous engagement that you have posted on YouTube. Include a biography, topics that you can talk about, and titles of some signature speeches you can give in a moment's notice.

   A page that shows your availability and expertise as a speaker allows event planners and others to see you speak and get a feel of what you will be like on stage. They like to see that you can actually engage with an audience.

4. Build the right relationships: Many business owners think they must speak at large

corporations or events to market their businesses effectively. This is not true. There are plenty of small groups that want to hear what you have to say. The most important thing is to have a clear target market and speak where they are going to be.

When you find some businesses, ask them what topics they want to hear about. Give them your one sheet and tell them that you are available to speak. If you have an engagement that is open to the public, send an email to contacts and invite them to come. If you add a video to your website, send a link with a not about the topic and video.

Someone you have been building a relationship with will have an opportunity for you to speak. You have been persistent, and they will think about you first.

5. Speak for free: When you first start to speak, you should do it for free. This could mean you

might have to speak free for years before you ever get your first paying gig.

Speaking for free gives you the expertise to be good enough to not charge for your speaking services but to speak at larger venues.

When you can start charging to speak, you will have good reasons to continue to speak for free. When you know that you will not be traveling for a while, send out emails to local contacts and let them know that you are in town and have time to speak.

For local gigs, offer a lower rate or do them for free especially if it is a group within your target market. You just might walk away with some new business.

PART 2

10 FUNDAMENTALS OF SOCIAL MEDIA MARKETING

Listening to Your Audience

One of the most important foundations of any marketing strategy is it social media or conventional marketing techniques, is listening to your target market. How do you listen? Many social media platforms nowadays provide 'Insights' which give you statistics of where they are their interests, who they are, what do they identify with and so on. Once you have gathered these details, you can create content that is tailored to their interests and needs and spark conversations that lead to sales.

Focusing on specialized content

Too much of fluff from any brand and you'll end up having people unfollow you or unsubscribe.

Specialized content is what you need here because it builds a strong brand. So instead of saying things like 'a one-stop solution for printing,' craft your message with something like 'exclusive purveyor of premium letterpress invitations and bespoke printing services.' Sounds classy, doesn't it**?**

You want quality, not quantity

Sure having 10,000 followers is a big deal but what if only 1,000 of them read, share, like and talk about your content? When you craft quality content, you'll attract quality readership and followers to your accounts, and these connections will not disappear.

Patience is Virtue

When you open a social media account, be ready to commit to the long haul to achieve quality followers. Sure you can pay for sponsored content, but when you first start your accounts, having generic views, likes and followers will help you understand who your targeted audience is, what sites they frequently visit, what hashtags they use and what are their spending habits.

Work to Build

Building an audience online is essential, and you'd get free publicity! If they like what they read, they'll share it with their own audiences whether it's through their own social media accounts or blogs and website. Sharing and discussing content enables you to reach new entry points and give Google more ways to find you. For example, if you type in natural skin care, the least likely brand to pop would be Sephora, but there it is, among the top 10 Google searches. You'd have thought that maybe Aesop or Kiehl's or even Origins would make a list. The reason why Sephora is up there is that of the many entries points their customer base chooses to associate the brand with their postings, comments, and images.

Social Media Influencers

Social Media Influencers, formerly known as bloggers are the people you want to associate your brand with. They already have the quality audiences, and they are most likely already interested in your product, business or service. Connect with them- don't shun them like what the Vogue editors did. Build relationships with your influencers- they will share your content with their followers, multiplying your reach and making your brand more down-to-earth and accessible.

Adding Value to your Conversation

If all you do is promote and promote your products and services, talk about your flash sales - people will stop listening. Part of social media marketing is also sharing, liking and being involved in topics related to your brand as well as jumping on the bandwagon of viral trends, political or social events that are happening in your country and in the world as well as corresponding to your audiences. You must add value to your online conversations and activities because this will develop relationships with your online audience.

Acknowledging your audience

Building online relationships is one of the surest ways to online marketing success. Sure there is no point reaching out to every person that tags you or comments- you might just create a storm! But once in awhile, where valid (and really use your discretion on this) it is proper to response to your audience especially when they've asked questions or have constructive suggestions.

Be Accessible

Publishing your content on the first week of the month and then not posting up anything for the next three months will not do you any favors. To be relevant and accessible, you need to post up content at a good pace. Be consistent but do not over-share (this can also cause you to lose your fan base). If followers see too little or too much from you, they will not hesitate to unfollow you. It only takes one click.

Create Reciprocity

In order to ensure your content is shared, you need to do the same for your influencers as well. A portion of the time you spend on social media should be given to sharing and talking about what other content that is being published on the world wide web, your influencers sites as well as your audiences.

CHAPTER 1: SOCIAL MEDIA MARKETING AND ITS IMPACT IN 2016

Back in 2013, social media marketing was something that most businesses and brands associated as a 'passing fad.' While having websites was high on the list, being active on social media was still something new and not a priority.

But at the same time, some entrepreneurs already saw the potential of social media marketing and considered it as the 'next big thing, ' and it must be taken advantage of, especially while it is still in the spotlight. However, to some, social media marketing didn't show any practical advantages it presented an unprofitable venture.

However, statistics from Hubspot showed a different kind of scenario. Two years ago, in 2014, 92% of businesses claimed that social media marketing proved to be extremely vital for their brands whereas a whopping 80% reported that social media activity increased traffic to their business's website.

To some entrepreneurs, social media marketing is the "next big thing," a temporary yet powerful fad that must be taken advantage of while it's still in the spotlight. But to a small selection of entrepreneurs, social media does not pose any practical benefits, and it comes with a complicated learning arc.

A poll conducted by Social Media Examiner in its sixth Social Media Marketing Industry Report showed that 97% of businesses participated in social media activities, but a total of 85% weren't exactly sure how best to use social media tools.

Not being sure of how to use social media is one thing but not using entirely thinking you can still do business the usual, old' fashioned way, is another thing.

The Impact of Online Reputation

Think about what you do before purchasing something in 2016? Do you go online and look for the company's website? Do you 'Google' them? The chances are that you do this. The phone book is obsolete- 'Googling' information is what it's all about now, and companies need to maintain a good online reputation as it creates the biggest impact on consumers.

Driving Traffic with Social Media

August 2015 came about, and Facebook announced

that it had 1.44 billion active users. That means, according to founder Mark Zuckerberg that one in seven people use Facebook to connect with brands, friends, and family. Facebook alone has a vast target audience. With each interaction and post on Facebook, there is a high potential of driving traffic to your site. This does not even include Instagram, Youtube, and Twitter yet. Developing and maintaining your social presence in 2016 will improve your relevance among the masses.

Cost Efficiency

The cost of social media marketing campaigns is one of the reasons why it is extensively used. Most profiles are free, and engagement with customers has no other expense except time. It takes less than a minute to post, comment or link. What's more, pay-per-click ads can be structured to target a specific demographics in a particular location!

Increasing Sales

In a recently conducted research, <u>one in every ten online purchases</u> globally came from social media platforms. Of course, this number is bound to grow bigger, even surpassing the $1 trillion dollar mark.

Social media postings are just as influential as television ads and what's more, it isn't as expensive as television or newspaper ads. A single non-paid ad on Twitter can engage millions of people that are interested in your product or your message.

Interaction on a Humanized Approach

Interaction in social media gives a platform for audiences and businesses to engage on an organic level, in other words- not forced. It also builds stronger ties and increases a trust in a brand. Social media also gives brands a human face- giving them personalities and making a brand more approachable, relatable and connected to the masses.

Mass Posting

If you have plenty of content to post up, companies can use certain tools such as Hootsuite, TweetDeck, SproutSocial and Buffer to distribute content across the different social media platforms simultaneously. This means that a marketer does not need to visit one site at a time to share a new post. Also, each social media now has the ability to sync making messages easier to post in real-time across a variety of platforms.

What Platforms Should you use?

The table below gives you a brief idea of what each social media is about and who should use to post what kind of content.

These are some of the most popular social media, but there are plenty more out there such as Tumblr, Snapchat, Periscope and so on.

It is always a good idea to explore each of these platforms because it is all unique in one way or another, however, for more traction, audience reach, and access, Facebook, Twitter and Instagram should be your top priority.

CHAPTER 2: SOCIAL MEDIA CASE STUDIES

Sometimes, the best way to learn things is by trial and error. Often, learning also takes place from observing others. The same can be said for social media. If you want to create a social media campaign, one of the first things you should do is some research. This research is required to find out what kinds of social media campaigns have brands, and companies conducted, how they have used the different types of social media as well as the best practices employed to get their message out to the masses. In this chapter, we will look at a few examples of how some businesses have used social media marketing to get their brand name out to the masses, increase sales and just connect with their audience:

Twitter

Bath Ales, a premium ale brand in the UK took to Twitter to conduct a campaign that ran from October 2010 to January 2011. Their objective with the campaign was simply to reach out and connect with their audience, especially loyal and long time fans of the ale. In this campaign, they urged Twitter users to tweet when they were drinking any of their ales and in return; Bath Ales would tweet back a thank you. This personal touch resonated with their audience and followers of their audience also drank the ales and twitted to Bath Ales. Sales increased by 56% during this period compared to the same time the year before when no social media activity took place. The cost of this campaign- low. The ROI received- impressive!

Use of Hashtags

With the use of #SausageSaturday hashtag, Heck Food kept their audience regularly updated with their line of sausages. They consistently posted messages related to the hashtag to maintain their customers enthused and inspire other ways of cooking sausages. These posting made the family-based brand more connected with their audiences, delivering a more family oriented brand image.

Starbucks also used Instagram and created their own general yet very specific hashtag- #redcupcontest. Hosting this for the second time in a row, Starbucks took to Instagram to check out customers Instagrams of the hashtag. This content received more than 40,000 entries. All customers had to do was tagging a photo with the hashtag and stand a chance to win prizes worth $500! The best part is, Starbucks did not specify if they had to drink a Starbucks drink, but Starbucks was the only one with the Red Cup.

Travel bag manufacturer, eBags also used the power of hashtags through the #TravelTipTuesdays to give their customers tips to make travel and packing easier. Their content is curated to provide useful advice on travel hygiene, packing and travels hacks and much more. This content went above, and beyond self-promotion and because of that, their audience was more open to sharing this content and thus widened their audience based.

Pinterest

One of the newest social media on the block, Pinterest is a great way of pinning everything and anything you see on the World Wide Web. Four Seasons Hotel, realizing the potential of the multitude of travel boards on Pinterest, created their own account and manages several beautiful boards related to travel destinations, travel fashion suggestions, bucket list suggestions, foodie tips and travel hacks, along with their own promotional content. The Four Seasons Pinterest page is an excellent way of using social media to connect with your audience in a non-promotional context.

Vine

Lowes loves Vines, and you can tell by their #fixinsix hashtag. Instead of using vines like how everyone does, Lowes creatively used Vines to share 6-second videos of cleaning, construction, and home improvement hacks. They gave out useful, substantial and concise content.

Instagram

The famous burrito makers took advantage of Instagram by allowing fans behind-the-scenes access to see the production line of their ingredients before they become burritos. Chipotle shows videos of avocados being made into guacamole, corn chips being salted, freshly washed jalapenos being sliced.

The videos reinforce Chipotle's message of preparing food with real and wholesome ingredients.

LinkedIn

Coca-Cola's LinkedIn Page *uses its LinkedIn page to post up content related to the* Coca-Cola Journey, *the soft drink company's digital magazine that produces over 2,000 stories since its November 2012 launch. The magazine has been a huge hit, especially on social media. The magazine's demographic is 59% of audience aged 18 to 35-year-old and receives a lot of interaction from its followers on Linkedin which has amassed over 1,107,008 followers. According to* Co-Managing Editor Jay Move, *LinkedIn is a major driving force for traffic for the company.* "That's obviously a different audience. It's a professional audience. It's professional social network versus more of a social network. We see great clickthrough rates on story links that we publish on LinkedIn. The percentage of clickthroughs is markedly higher than it is on Facebook, and to a degree, Twitter." With the professional audience in mind, The Coca-Cola team choose to share its magazine content on LinkedIn, thriving on the site's consumer-focused groups, business innovations, workplace details, and jobs.

Snapchat

Conceptualized in 2011, Snapchat became a hit by 2012. Some of the most important users and uses of Snapchat was by political candidates such as Bernie Sanders and Hillary Clinton that used SnapChat in 2015 to reach a younger audience. Hillary Clinton, for example, took a Snapchat of her #justchilling. This marks the first time where politicians have used Snapchat as part of their campaign marketing initiatives.

These case studies show the enormous potential that social media marketing can do for any business depending on what these business needs are from reaching out to a new set of audience, expanding the audience, connecting with existing clientele and increasing profits.

Here's a look at some of the benefits that social media marketing can do to improve your business statistics:

Heightened Levels of Brand Recognition

Every opportunity to increase your brand's visibility is valuable. With social media networks, you now have new channels to voice out your brand's voice and content without relying on conventional channels such as the television and newspaper. Social media provides an easier way for your audience to access you and it makes it easier for you to access new audience- it works both ways. A Facebook user could have stumbled on your business by seeing their friend like one of your posts. A Twitter user could've heard about your company by clicking on a trending hashtag. A dormant customer could be more acquainted with your products or services after seeing your brand pop up everywhere.

Increased Brand Loyalty

Brands that engage in social media read the rewards of higher brand loyalty. A recent report by the Texas Tech University stated that a strategic and open source social media plan could help in changing mindsets and increase brand loyalty. Starbucks for example still remains a force on Twitter, ranking in #4 in the Top 100 Twitter Brands. Starbucks remains in the top 10 because they are constantly engaging with their customers. Their tweets are either replies to individual tweets or re-posts of their consumer's tweets. One and off you'll see targeted promotional Starbucks material. In essence, Starbucks is listening to what their customers are talking about and giving feedback whenever necessary.

Increase the Opportunities of Conversion

With every post you make, every video you post, every link you share and every like you give- you open up the opportunities for customers to convert to your brand. With social media, you need to build a following, and when you do, you open up access to recent customers and new customers, and you'll be able to interact with the, through posts, images, videos, and comments. For every post, there is also a reaction that could lead to a website visit, a purchase of a product or even a re-tweet to a whole new customer base.

Just take note that not all reactions result in a site visit, but every positive reaction or interaction leads to a possible conversion down the pipeline. Opportunity is present at any given time when it comes to social media so always be sure to react when you can!

Increase the Human Approach

With social media, brands create a face and personality and also a more humanized approach in their interactions. Social media is the place where brands can act like people, and this is crucial because everyone likes doing business with other people and not with companies. A survey done by State of Inbound Marketing showed that social media generates a 100% higher lead-to-close ratio than outbound marketing. The statistics shown at Hubspot.com also showed that people are more trusting towards brands that have a strong social media presence.

@Oreo

Stronger Brand Authority

Brands that regularly interact with their customers project good faith. When a client receives excellent service (or bad service), gets a fantastic or faulty product- they had to social media to compliment or air their grievances. When these customers link your brand name to the post, others will want to follow you for more updates because their friend experienced fantastic service. Similarly, if they complain- you'd lose out on customers too. Interacting with major influences or other brands on social media also increases your authority.

Higher Inbound Traffic

Before social media, your inbound traffic was limited to only the people already on your clientele list and the person who come looking for you after a keyword search. But with social media, you create several different paths leading back to your site because every piece of content that you syndicate creates a pathway for a new customer or visitor to approach you. Make sure what you are syndicating is quality content because this will create quality inbound traffic which will lead to more conversions and more leads.

Reduced Marketing Expenditure

Well, social media is fast becoming the preferred marketing tool as it requires little money to generate increased traffic. One hour a day spent on developing your social media content and syndication strategy could give you higher analytical information, in real time of your efforts. Paid advertising on Facebook is also significantly cheaper than conventional advertising needs.

If you plan on going through with social media marketing, then create a plan and a budget and start small. Once you get the hang of it, you can increase your budget and your conversion rates simultaneously.

Better SEO Rankings

SEO still ranks as the best way to capture relevant traffic from search engines whoever the success rates are changing. Hub post reports that '60% of all organic clicks go to the organic top 3 search results' whereas the Search Engine Journal states that SEO searches lead to a 14.6% close rate. While it is worthwhile to keep your blogs and websites constantly optimized with title tags and meta descriptions, it is no longer enough. Google and other search engines also calculate rankings based on social media presence as a major contributing factor to SEO, and this is crucial if you want a strong brand. Your activity on social media creates a brand signal to search engines, telling them that your brand is legitimate, trustworthy and credible. Nowadays, keywords aren't only important- a strong social media presence is mandatory.

Better Customer Experiences

Social media presents another line of communication just like newsletters, emails, and phone calls. But with social media, you are creating a public demonstration of customer service, and when other people see this, you, in turn, enrich your relationships with your existing customers.

Complaints should be immediately addressed (again, where appropriate as there are too many online trolls)., action should be taken to make things right again.

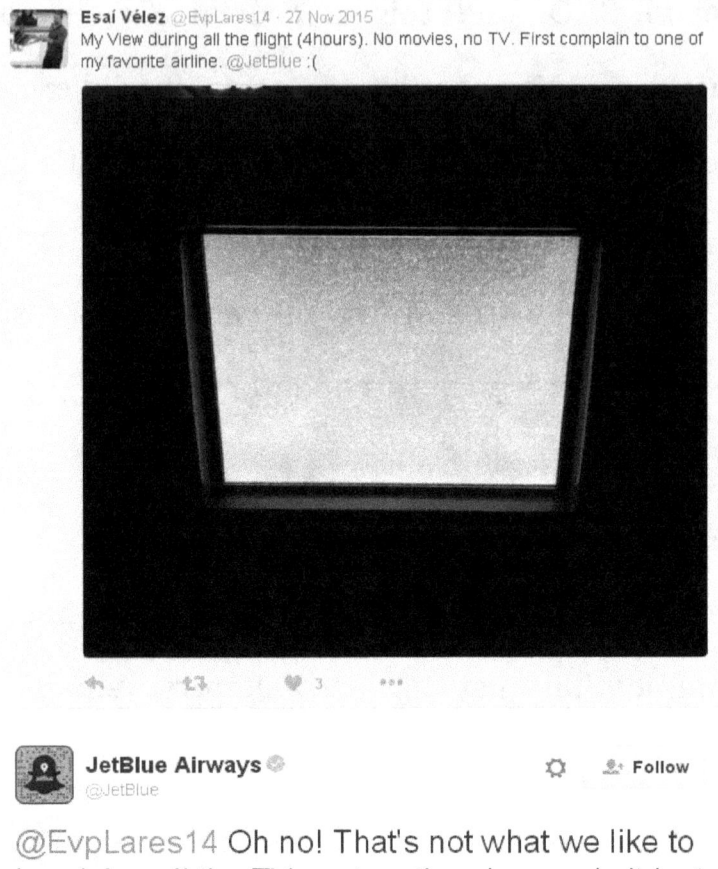

And if you get compliments from your customers, thank them! Personal experiences from the brand's customers will let them know you care about them.

Better Insights

Facebook & Instagram and even Twitter provide Insights which track user interaction on your social media platforms. If can help you track the number of active users, so you have a better idea of what content performs well. Tracking their behaviors and their interests is calls social listening. This helps you track what people think of your business and see what type of content generates the most interests, likes, and shares. This will help you gain more valuable insight into what your audience reacts too, and you can craft your content to provide them with more of these interesting information.

The Bottom Line

There is no saying that social media is a passing fad. Even if it, it won't cause you much to open some of the most popular accounts such as Facebook and Instagram to share your business to the masses.

If you aren't convinced enough, here are a few more push points to drive the social media marketing point home:

- Your competition is already doing it- why aren't you? If your competitors are on social media, this would mean your potential web traffic is being directed and converted to their sites. Do not let your competitors read the benefits while you prevent yourself from being innovative.
- This is your opportunity to build relationships- the Gen X of the world today is one of the highest categories of workers, and they are all on social media. You need to create relationships with them and to grow if you

plan on staying in the business for long. The sooner you start, the better you will get at building your audiences so do not wait.

- There's nothing to lose- social media is free to use unless you start on paying for adverts. But it takes minimal effort to learn and get involved in. The amount of time and money you invest into your social media accounts is relatively minimal compared to conventional marketing channels such as ads in the newspaper or magazine. You stand to gain a higher rate of conversion and publicity just by being active even on one social media account.

At this day and age, things are moving so fast. What was viral one week ago would be forgotten the next so jump on the bandwagon on social media marketing as fast as you can because otherwise, you'd lose out even more.

Social media marketing, done right can lead to more sales, more customers, more traffic and more conversions.

CHAPTER 3: SOCIAL MEDIA ACCOUNTS - WHAT'S BEST FOR YOUR BUSINESS

It's 2016 now, and by this time, you probably have a pretty good idea or a vague sense of what social media is all about.

Social media is a collection of online, Internet-based communication channels that thrive on community-based interactions, input, collaboration, and content-sharing.

Forums such as OffTopic and 4Chan, micro-blogging sites such as Tumblr social networking sites such as Facebook and social bookmarking sites such as Digg and social curation sites like Reddit and Wikis are the various types of social media that people can use.

Prominent Social Media Platforms to use

FACEBOOK

Facebook is one of the most popular and free social networking sites that allow users to create profiles upload content from photos and videos and send messages, pokes to friends and keep in touch with people on Facebook. To open an account, all you need to do is go to www.facebook.com and click on sign up. Next, put in your first name, surname, a mobile number or an email address and your password. You are also required to fill in your birthday and identify your gender.

Once you're done, Facebook will send in a verification email to the email address that you have inserted to verify your account, and just like that, you are a registered Facebook user!

When we talk about Social Media marketing, Facebook has a special account catered to businesses, and this is called Pages. To open a Facebook page, you must first have a private Facebook account, and in this case, it's the account you opened up earlier. This is your own personal Facebook account- your Pages account is exclusively for your business.

How to open a Facebook Page?

Below mentioned is a series of simple steps to follow

to open a Facebook page.

Step 1- Choose a Page Type

Head on over to https://www.facebook.com/pages/create.php. You need to click on what selection best fits your business needs. These types are:

1. Local Business or Place
2. Company, Organization, or Institution
3. Brand or Product
4. Artist, Band, or Public Figure
5. Entertainment
6. Cause or Community

If you are a business that serves your community, then no1 is your best category, but if your business serves a whole county or the entire world, then no2 is your category. Since we are talking about Social Media Marketing, for this tutorial, let us focus on option no.2- Company, Organization or Institution.

When you click on Company, Organization or Institution, Facebook will require you to specify the type of your company by choosing a category. This can be anything from a political organization, food & beverage, community organization, Preschool, School, Small Business or Travel and Leisure.

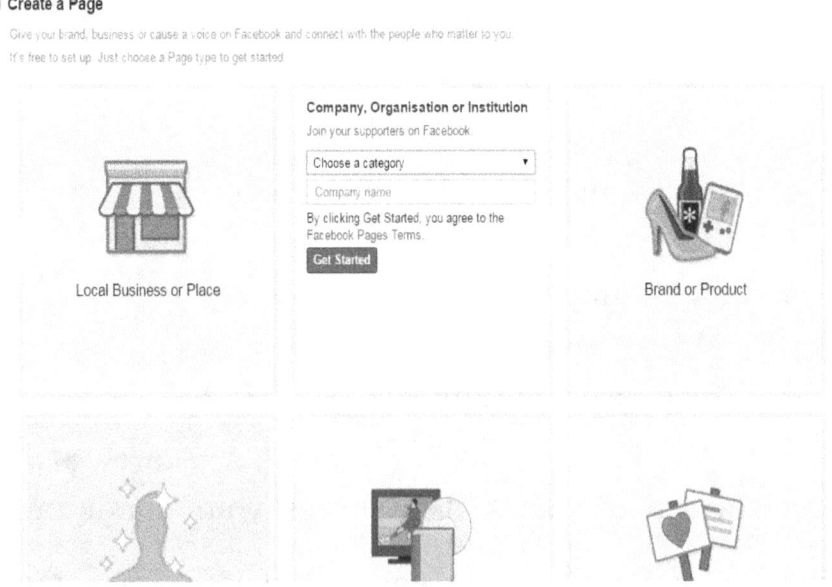

You are also required to provide a company name. We recommend that you follow exactly the business name that you have registered it under. Facebook allows you only to change your business name and URL once, so make sure you make the right choice.

Step 2- Fill in the Basic Information

By completing the first step, Facebook will then automatically walk you through four primary sections of information which will provide the foundations of your Page. You need to give a short description of your company within two to three sentences. This will be the main introduction to your site. Make sure that this information is the same as what is shown on your website or your objectives. The great thing is, the contents on the About page can be revised.

Personalize your URL so that it's easier to promote your Facebook page on other materials and sites as well as on your website. A confusingly long URL isn't going to make it. The URL should mirror your Page's name or Business name. For example, if your business is Delia's Homemade Cakes then your URL can be www.facebook.com.deliascakes

A profile picture is a must so being a business page, uploading a logo for your business is the right step. Your profile picture will serve as the first visual icon for your page so make it identifiable and the same with all your other online presence because you want to increase brand recognition. Anything you publish on your page or comments to other sites will have your profile picture. A square image works best, in the size of 180 x 180 pixels.

Fill in your contact details and include a cover photo as well. Once you are done, Facebook will also prompt you to advertise your new page. However, do not do this immediately- regardless if paid advertisement is part of your strategy or not. There is no point having paid advertisement when you do not have compelling content on your page. So before you click to subscribe, work on getting relevant material on your page first.

Step 3- Getting Acquainted with the Admin Panel

The good thing about Facebook is that it is extremely user-friendly. Once you are done including all the relevant information, you are one step ahead of providing a solid foundation for your Page. Your Business Page is now LIVE! But don't share it to your personal feed or suggest it to your friend's list. You do not want to do any of these until you get good content up.

On you, page, look for your 'Settings.' Click it, and you will see two panels. On the left are the various setting categories and on the right are the different items you can edit or change. Here the most important things that you need to change/edit or add are the Page Info which basically tells people about your business. You can also change the Notifications to determine how you'd like to receive Page alerts and most importantly is the Page Roles. This function allows you to decide who the primary manager of the Page should be, who can be editors or contributors.

Step 4- Adding Strategic Content

When it comes to content, Facebook allows six different types of content uploads which are:

1. Plain text status
2. Photo with caption
3. Link with caption
4. Video with caption
5. Event page

6. Location check-in

For the first post, go with a status update to say hello and perhaps an update on the latest project that you are working on. Down the road of your social media marketing campaign, be sure to use a variety of content to engage, educate and connect with your audience.

Once you are done with uploading your profile photo, make sure to update your cover photo too. The cover photo helps attract people to your Page.

Now that you have content on your page, you can invite friends first, then your colleagues and your acquaintance whom you know can create some primary activity. You can also encourage your customers now that you have some form of activity on your page.

Step 5: Measure your Progress

Insights by Facebook are a great tool for Facebook Pages. This feature allows you to monitor the activity of your visitors based on the content you have uploaded. You get to see the page views, page likes, reach and engagement over a certain period of time. You can also see what activity is:

- Organic : the number of people who visited/clicked/liked/shared/viewed your post without unpaid distribution
- Paid: the number of people who visited/liked/clicked/shared/viewed your post as a result of viewing your ads

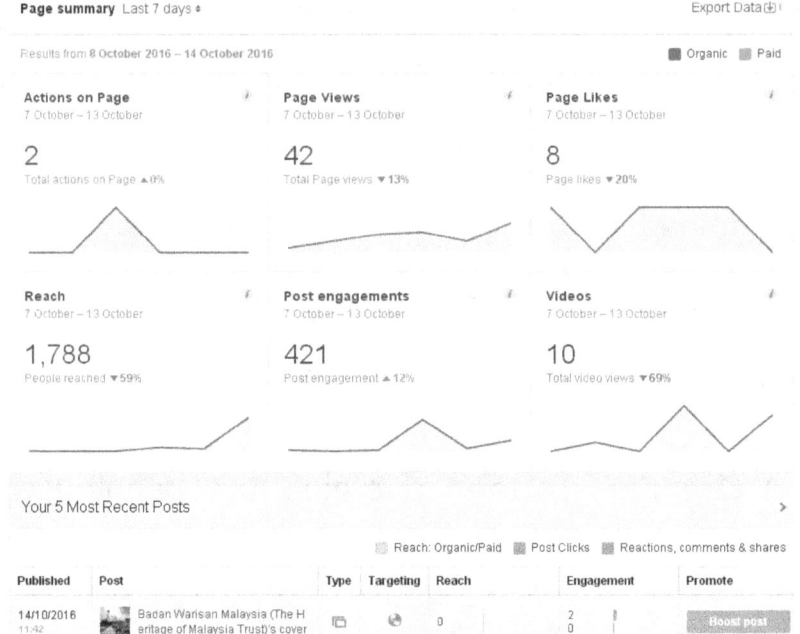

Insights will also tell you which posts have a higher engagement, reach and the time with the highest activity. All this valuable data will enable you to craft future messages to target an even greater correspondence. It will also tell you which items work and which don't.

With Insights you can view:

- **Overview:** This tab shows you the overall activity within a 7-day timeline such as page likes, post reach, and overall visitor engagement.
- **Likes:** This tab will show you the growth and losses of your fan base. You will also see what how paid posts and organic posts have performed.
- **Reach:** This tab shows you the organic number of people your posts or page reaches every day. Once a week, check this statistic to see if there are spikes in your data and cross-check it to see what you posted that day.
- **Views:** This tab tells you where your visitors are coming from- as in from another website, an article mentioning your business, another Facebook account and so on.

And with that, you now have a Facebook Page!

TWITTER

Twitter, founded in March 2006 is a free microblogging platform that enables its users to post up 140 character messages, aptly called 'tweets.' Opening up a Twitter account is similar to opening up a Facebook account.

Below mentioned is a series of simple steps to follow to open a Twitter account for business.

Step 1: Create A Twitter Account

Head to https://twitter.com/ . At the landing page, fill up the details in the Sign-Up form.

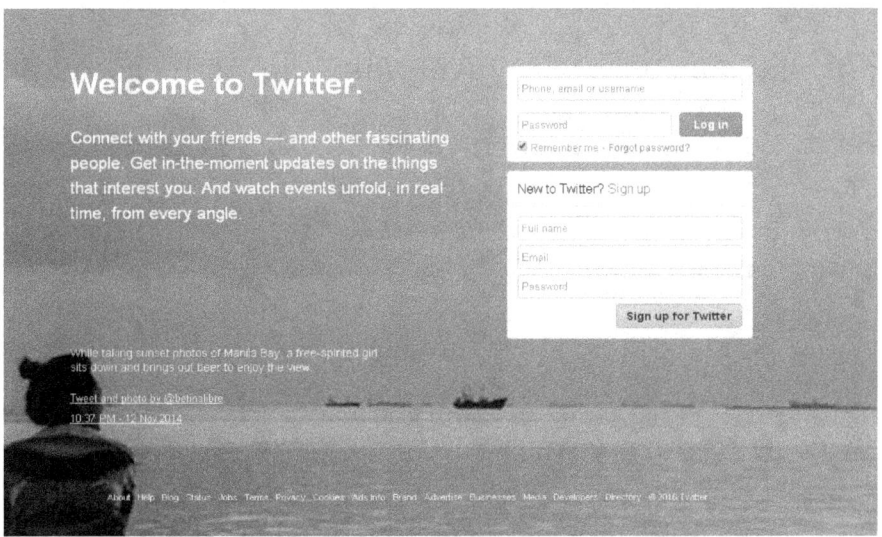

This should be the same details you used when you opened your Facebook account. Of course, your password can be different if you like. Enter your business Name and work email when required. While these features can be changed, take note that you want it to be easily identifiable with your business, so if your Facebook page is Delia's Homemade Cupcakes, then your Twitter handle should be something like @deliascakes. You want something that that is easy to remember and searchable for your customers. You also need it to be short because when someone tags you in their posts, your username will take up the character limit. So keep usernames short for this reason.

Step 2: Create your Profile

Once you have completed with verifying your account, you need to set your profile too. It's the same as Facebook where you need to upload a profile picture as well as a header image (called a cover photo on Facebook). Before you add people or follow anyone on Twitter, you want them to have something to look at in your profile. Essentially, Twitter has made it easy for people to create their

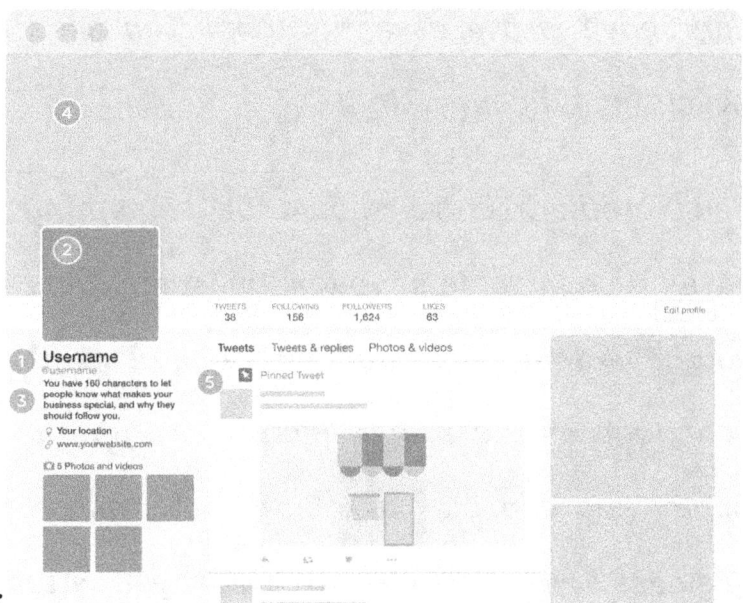

profile:

1- Username

2- Profile Picture

3- Short Description

4- Header image

5- Your Pinned Tweet

The above is five essential items you need to start tweeting and connecting!

Your profile picture should be something that is easily recognizable so follow the same thing as what you have done with your Facebook account and use your logo as the profile picture. As for the header photo, you can pick anything that represents your business, whether it's an event you attended or organized, a group picture with your customers or a picture of your store front.

In your profile, add your contact details as well your website. You can also link your Facebook and any other social media accounts by going to Settings> Applications and connecting your profiles.

Step 3: Connecting with your customers

Just like Facebook, Twitter is also about connecting with other users. Twitter is great to build new connections and networks, as you'll receive recommendations on who to follow from athletes to celebrities to business leaders, influencers, and politicians. You can select to follow who you want according to your business needs.

Step 4: Send you Tweets!

Well, you've got your profile up, and you are following some excellent influencers so now it's time to send a shout out to the world! Aim to be as concise as you can. If you are adding links, Twitter automatically shortens the links for you. While internet lingo is creative, you really want to set a tone for your tweets so while it's great to keep up with what is lit at the moment, you ought to slow down the 'slay' a little bit and keep the tone slightly business casual, especially if it's a business page. Abbreviations such as ICYMI or TBT or BTW are fine but don't start with 'ur' or 'cuz' or 'fo sho.'

First your first tweet, you can use the ever popular hashtag #myfirstTweet. All you need to do is hit the 'Tweet' button, and you're off! Here are some examples of first tweets:

1. Is this thing on? So, what shall we talk about?
   Arby's (@Arbys) June 29, 2010

2. Welcome, all of our Wendy's fans to our new page!
   Wendy's (@Wendys) July 27, 2009

3. Welcome to Starbucks Twitter land!
   Starbucks Coffee (@Starbucks) August 12, 2008

4. I have awoken! Time to tweet the rainbow.
   Skittles (@Skittles) February 4, 2010

5. If You Have A Body, You Are An Athlete. -Bill Bowerman http://t.co/PPE1BSs8

    Nike (@Nike) December 29, 2011

6. I'm 01100110 01100101 01100101 01101100 01101001 01101110 01100111 00100000 01101100 01110101 01100011 01101011 01111001 00001010

    A Googler (@google) February 26, 2009

7. Warren is in the House

    Warren Buffett (@WarrenBuffett) 2 May 2013 https://twitter.com/HBO/statuses/3981482454

Step 5: Don't Forget to engage!

Twitter is a great channel to engage with your customers! You can either retweet or follow back some of your customers, or you can also answer questions! Regularly tweeting from your profile is by far one of the best ways to reach your audience as you will create good content on your site.

Another way to ensure your content reaches the different groups of your customers is by syncing your accounts. Now that you have Facebook, any tweet you post will also be posted on your Facebook Page! This will ensure that customers who have only either one account still receive your messages and content.

Try to schedule tweets at least once in two days and work on doing this at a specific time.

Twitter also has the Facebook equivalent of Insights, called Analytics which enables you to track your engagement levels and learn how to make your Tweets more successful. It also gives you information on your audience's interests, locations as well as demographics.

To enable Analytics, go to your Logo Icon on the right side of the screen and from the drop down menu, choose Analytics.

Meet your dashboards

Tweet activity — Measure engagement and learn how to make your Tweets more successful.

Followers — Explore the interests, locations, and demographics of your followers.

Twitter Cards — Track how your Twitter Cards drive clicks, app installs, and Retweets.

Click on 'turn analytics on' to see your impressions, engagements and engagement rate. Analytics also allows you to export this information via the 'Export Data' feature.

Engaging on Twitter also means collaborating with other influencers. With the right connections, you can receive shout-outs on their sites, and you can also do a friendly promotion on your site! You want to showcase your brand personality when you connect and tweet so the more you tweet, the more engaged you will be with your users.

INSTAGRAM

Apart from Facebook and Twitter, Instagram is also a must have option in your social media marketing repertoire. With over 500 million monthly active users, your business can definitely tap into this huge market segment. A recent study showed that only 36% of marketers actually use Instagram for business compared to a whopping 93% on Facebook. So essentially, you have a significant market that is untapped on Instagram whereas Facebook and Twitter are oversaturated and highly competitive.

Instagram is a great option if you want to push

through all that clutter. To get started, follow the steps below to create and blast out your account and content on Instagram:

Step 1: Setting Up An Instagram Account

Unlike Facebook or Twitter that allows you to create an account via a Web browser, the easiest way to set up an Instagram account is by downloading the app to your smartphone. Having an Instagram account can be a tricky choice to make that is why not many marketers use it. So it'd be nice if you can define the purpose of your channel. Think about:

- Do you want to extend the reach of your brand? Or do you just want to create a place where your customers can share pictures of your products?
- Do you want to highlight a different perspective of your brand? Attract new talent?

If you feel you need inspiration, then you can always check other businesses out and see if they have an Instagram account and what they post up on it.

Many Instagrammers have become celebrities showcasing their makeup, fitness, cake making and even photographs. For example, if your business is Delia's Homemade Cupcakes, then an Instagram account to showcase how you make these cupcakes is a great idea!

To set up your account, again, you need to create an account name to match your business. Stick with the same Username you have given for your Twitter account- @deliascakes.

Your bio should also be short and again, use the same as what you have done on Twitter. Why? Because you want brand recognition and the same message to go out regardless of the platform, you are using. In your bio, be sure to put in your website link too.

Instagram's business profile allows users to add contact information and business address as well as specify the category of your business. Again, when you open up your Instagram account, it will ask you if you'd like to link it with your Facebook account- agree to this because all info from Facebook will be automatically transferred to your Instagram accounts such as business information and contact options.

Step 2: Creating Great Content

The great thing about Instagram is that it is all about visuals. Your content must be visually attractive to add value to your audience and future customers. Use Instagram to inspire, entertain and educate and not always about promoting your product or service. Instagram allows the upload of:

-Videos of up to 1 minute

-Images in square format

Use hashtags and great captions to accompany your photos. The great thing about Instagram is that it is a very youthful and fun vibe so you can create captions that aren't so business formal. A little bit of sass and some cool words will really drive up your views.

A great motto for Instagram is 'If your brand were a person, how would you describe its personality?'

Here are some great examples of how brands have used Instagram to create a personality for their brand:

HomeGoods

HomeGoods uses Instagram to combine decorating tips while showcasing how their products can be used in a very personal way.

 homegoods

HomeGoods Welcome to our showcase of customer finds. Tag a HomeGoods item in your photo with #foundathomegoods and you could get a regram too.
www.homegoods.com

1,401 posts   **1.7m** followers   **3,173** following

National Geographic

Lorna Jane

Lorna Jane's Instagram posts feature women who represent their customer's persona. Their posts are inspirational, playful, colorful, powerful and active, embodying the brand's essence.

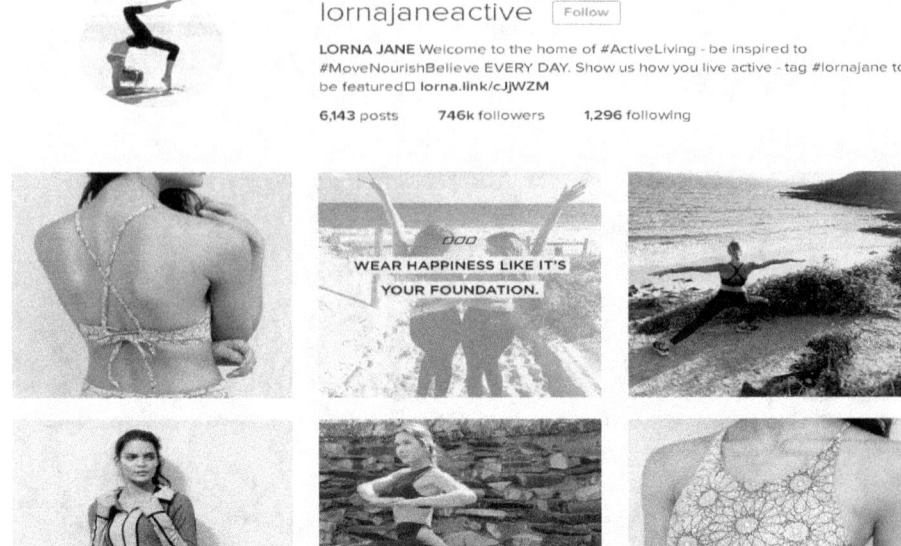

Try as best as you can to accompany each image with a caption and hashtags. Hashtags help expand your reach.

Step 3: Engage with others brands, influencers and create relationships

Engaging with relevant influencers can do wonders for your brand. You may also want to collaborate with other brands that you often do business with.

For example, if your business is to make cupcakes, then you may want to work with your baking supplier! Use their ingredients or baking equipment and tag them. Instagram is a great platform to showcase your team spirit, making you more likable, humanized and approachable.

Just recently, Instagram also has its own Insights! Just like Twitter's and Facebook's Insights, users can track things like total reach, and impressions click to the link in your bio as well as the percentage of followers who are male or female! You can also get an idea of their location (which part of the world) and even the exact city.

LINKEDIN

LinkedIn, the professional equivalent of Facebook with 380 million members and at least <u>4 million company pages</u>, LinkedIn has grown leaps and bounds over the last 14 years since its inception in 2002.

By now, every professional who's got a page or account with LinkedIn knows that it is not just a social media platform to engage and connect. LinkedIn is this and so much more. LinkedIn's unique approach to content marketing made it noticeable with influencers who want to share and engage via content distribution rather than just merely looking for

Content marketing advantage for social media has shown that influencers aren't just going to LinkedIn to find jobs. Nope, they are there to share and engage with other professionals, job seekers and influences. By this time, you would already have a good idea of how to open profiles, assuming that by now, you've already opened Facebook, Instagram, and Twitter.

In this section regarding LinkedIn, we will focus on how to optimize your LinkedIn Business Page.

Step 1: Optimizing for Users and Search Purposes

This of your LinkedIn profile just as you would your company website. Your LinkedIn Page represents your brand. In optimizing your LinkedIn page, there are three fundamentals that you need to look at:

Consistency

Consistency is essential when it comes to how you present yourself online and offline. Your branding collateral regarding your message, voice, personality and corporate design need to be in-sync across all profiles.

Accuracy

Whatever figures or stats, links or facts that you post up on LinkedIn needs to be accurate because your LinkeIn audience is not just any audience. LinkedIn is full of highly educated and influential groups of people.

Semantics

Anything at all that you post up on your social media accounts, especially on LinkedIn shows up in search results, so apart from being careful what you post up, you should also optimize your LinkeIn Page with identifying keywords- keywords that you've used on your website as well your social media pages. You can also use industry-specific keywords to target your LinkedIn audience; bearing in mind that they are a lot more sophisticated than the audiences on other social media sites.

Step 2: Optimizing your LinkedIn Profile

There are several sections that you want to use targeted keywords to optimize your LinkedIn profile such as the 'Products and Services' section as well as the 'Careers' section. At these sections, you want to pay more attention to the words for the titles, subtitles of course as well as the copy of the page. Each of these elements as a whole must be consistent, accurate, and consistent and project your brand personality.

Authentic and high-quality content is what will give you organic reach, and this is what ultimately matters. When you get visitors via organic search and reach- whether through a LinkedIn search or a direct visit, your content must be compelling and targeted to continue engaging users. The real results on your content will be measured by the clicks you receive from your audience on the content on your page and what actions they take as your content directs them to.

Step 3: Expand Your Social Reach

As much as it's easy to use ads to build your social network reach fast, without knowing where you stand in keyword research and compelling content is no use. Growing your reach in LinkedIn is the same with building your reach with Twitter, Facebook or Instagram.

So what do you need to do to add followers to your LinkedIn page?

According to a survey done at BrightEdge, there was a positive connection between the numbers of employees to the number of LinkedIn followers. Every company that was among the top 100 brands had a greater percentage of their staff on LinkedIn than the number of followers. The top 10 brands had at least 60% of their employees on LinkedIn.

What does this mean for marketers?

Here's where you invest in your employees. Get them to set up their LinkedIn profiles, identifying themselves as your company's employees. Step back and wait to see if this has an impact on your network —if it's working, then reinforce or double your efforts. More people will be attracted to your organization when they see your employees identifying with your company. This will also increase your messages and updates.

Step 4: Create And Share Your Page's content

Search engines will search for the keywords that are connected to you, and awesome content will show up in search results and on other sites. Your content should be engaging to its targeted audience. So how do you continue to hold your audience interested and engaged in your brand?

Share Updates Often

To constantly maintain an ongoing interest in your company, you need to continue posting up relevant content on a timely basis to connect and engage with your followers and influencers. Updates can be anything related directly or indirectly to your company, best practices, leadership material, and industry news and job openings.

Remember always to stick to what users will care about most and try to share as much relevant and useful content as possible. Relevance and uniqueness of content are much more important than the number of postings.

Create Inspiring, Relevant and Creative Content

Create content based on what's happening at the time. When Kim Kardashian achieved a cover picture with Time Magazine, LinkedIn published a post on how to successfully market yourself just the way Kim does.

What does this mean for you?

Every time you feel an international event has a direct relationship to your company, write something about it. It doesn't have to be industry related news all the time. It can be related to something such as 'How Hurricane Matthew will impact sustainable travel' for instance or even "10 things I learned as an intern'.

Link Social Profiles

It's an obvious best practice to connect you social media profiles with your LinkedIn ones. Cross-platform linking will help the sharing of content across multiple interest ranges, thus reaching a wider audience.

Step 5: Encourage Recommendations

The number of recommendations seen on a page is similar to the number of likes a Facebook page gets. Recommendations are like the word-of-mouth of the online version. When you are selecting a partner company to work with, many marketers look to LinkedIn for social proof. Recommendations on Linkedin tell your visitors what products and services you have to offer, but it also tells you how amazing you describe yourself in your products and services section. Try to get as many recommendations as you can from customers, associates, and business partners- it builds trust.

YOUTUBE

YouTube is among the most popular search engines people use, coming in second after Google. More than just a video-sharing platform, YouTube is also the third most popular website in the world, with at least three billion unique visitors each month.

Thinking of using YouTube as part of your social media marketing arsenal? Well, it can definitely improve your search engine rankings. Here's a rundown of how you can use YouTube for Business:

Setting up your YouTube Account

YouTube channels are easy to open. As long as you have a Gmail address, you have a YouTube account, but that doesn't mean you have a channel. Follow the steps found here:

https://support.google.com/youtube/answer/1646861?hl=en to help you start a YouTube channel. You will also be asked to verify your account through your mobile device.

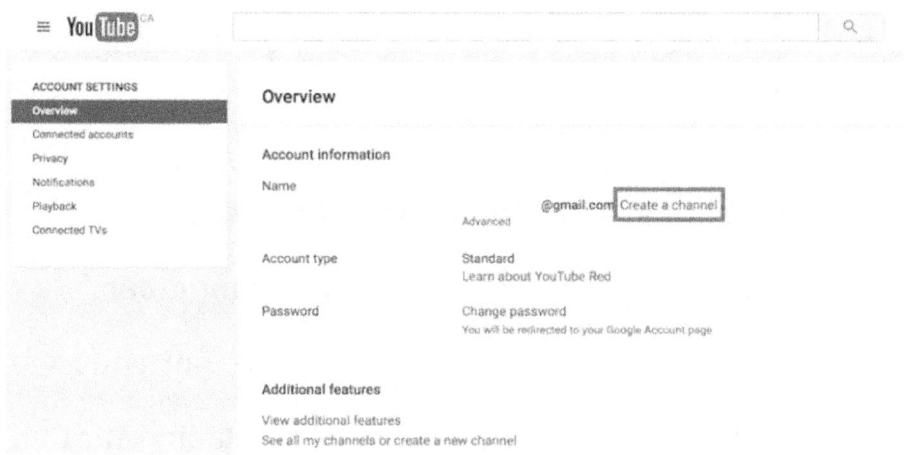

Again, when selecting your username and Channel name, always use your business name or the usernames that you have chosen for your other accounts.

In the case of this book, we started off with Facebook, Instagram, Twitter and LinkedIn. So,

Facebook: Delia's Homemade Cakes URL: www.facebook.com.deliascakes

Instagram: @deliascakes

Twitter: @deliascakes

YouTube: Delia's Homemade Cakes URL:

www.facebook.com.deliascakes

In your channel description, copy the content you have made for your Facebook page. Remember, consistency is king! In your description, put your website URL at the top as opposed to placing it at the bottom because people will less likely see it.

You also get to choose a specific category for your channel.

Create a new channel

Name your channel

Select a category

Your new channel comes with a Google+ page

I agree to the Pages Terms

Done

Upload videos
Upload public and private videos to your new channel

Join the conversation
Comment on videos using your channel name

All across Google
Your new channel comes with a Google+ page

Branding Identity

Just like Facebook, LinkedIn, and Twitter, you can also personalize your channel by changing your background image and use a theme color. Use the same logo as you did for your other social channels as well as an engaging background image to go to your YouTube Channel. It can be the same as you used for Facebook or LinkedIn but it can also be something different, and youthful.

Video Length

By default, you are allowed a maximum of 15 minutes for each video, but if you want to increase your limit, you can go to YouTube's video upload page to increase it. However, longer videos don't mean it's better. At this day and age where people want to see videos and get information fast, long videos will result in your audience losing focus because they don't have enough patience. Most viewed videos have been 5 minutes or fewer.

When you do start on YouTube, make snappy, small videos that give your messages our succinctly, focused and straight to the point.

Video Types

Your content on your Youtube channel really has to be all about you so tailor it to target your current clients, prospective clients, and fans. Your videos should be serving their needs, but videos that look and sound like commercials have a lower percentage to be shared. Tips on decorations, DIYs, how-tos, home improvement, marketing techniques, design ideas and basically information people can immediately use usually content that will be shared. Your audience makes a split second decision to share so position yourself as the expert in your industry and use your Youtube channel as a long-term public relations campaign.

After Uploading Your Video

Video titles also increase your SEO and SMO (social media optimization) so remember to put a title that is descriptive and compelling. For the description of the video, optimize it with specific keywords that your target audience will be typing into search what they are looking for. Make use of the tags that give more description to your video content because search engines will pick this up. Pick specific ones as well as general overviews.

Sharing Your Video

When you are doing with uploading your video, make sure to share it on your other channels! This will help you reach your audience much faster and get your content seen! The share button below your video will enable you to share on the relevant platforms:

You can also copy the link and insert it in a newsletter or upload it to your website.

Analytics and Reports

Like Facebook, Twitter and Instagram, YouTube also has its own analytics so you can see your particular states and information on your viewer's activity on your channel. Here, you can see the top 10 most watched videos as well as playback locations. On each video, there is also a 'statistics' link that will show you the age, device used and operating systems of their device. These metrics will help you cater to your audience by providing more targeted content.

CHAPTER 4: DOING SOCIAL MEDIA MARKETING THE RIGHT WAY

Social Media Marketing, or for short, SMM is a form of internet-based marketing that incorporates a verity of social media networks to achieve branding and marketing targets and goals.

SMM involves the activities of sharing content, videos, and images socially, for marketing purposes. Brian Solis, a digital analyst, author, and speaker created a social media chart known as The Conversation Prism to categorize social platforms into various services and types of social media. (See a larger image)

Social media is an essential component of a person's online life. With each New Year, there are new social websites and applications that make social communication even more profound. Businesses use social media to promote brands, market products, connect with customers, expand reach and influence and build new business ties.

The following is a variety of terms commonly associated with social media marketing and it is essential to know what they mean so you would be able to use them in your online marketing campaign:

Social Media Analytics- one of the primary reasons why social media marketing is an arsenal for any marketer is the fact that data can be obtained easily and quickly. Social Media analytics is all about gathering data from social media websites and blogs. This data is analyzed to enable marketers to make better decisions for their businesses and brands. Social media analytics is commonly used to assess customer sentiment towards a product or service and how their reactions can support marketing and customer service activities. Social Media marketing reaps the benefits of social networking to enable a company to increase its brand recognition and presence as well as expand their customer reach. Social Media Marketing's goal is also to continuously stay relevant by creating compelling content that will prompt users to share what they have to say on their own social networks.

Social Media Marketing also includes social media optimization (SMO), and it works like how SEO, search engine optimization is except with SMO, the main goal is to attract unique visitors to a website via social networks.

There are two ways of handling SMO which are:

1- Adding social media links to content such as 'Tweet it' buttons, RSS feeds, sharing buttons, Pin It buttons
2- Promoting activities through social media via tweets, pins, blog posts and status updates

Social CRM, also known as Social Customer Relationship Marketing is another powerful business tool that marketers use. When a visitor to your social network 'likes' or 'follows' you, this opens up a host of communication, marketing, and networking opportunities. Social media sites enable a customer to follow conversations about your company and brand in real-time, and the company receives market data and feedback.

Social Media CRM works both ways. It enables a customer to tell a company and everyone about their experiences with the company's products or services, both good and bad experiences. For the business perspective, it enables them to respond in real-time to both these positive and negative feedback, attend to customer problems almost immediately as well as rebuild or regain customer confidence. How a brand reacts is imperative to the overall future and growth of a company.

Enterprise Social Networking, on the other hand, allows a company to connect people who have similar business interests or activities. For a company's employees, it enables them to access resources and information that they would require to work together effectively and solve business issues and problems.

Public social media platforms also enable businesses to stay connected with their customers, and it makes it easier for them to conduct research where this data can be used to enhance their business process and operations.

Crowdsourcing Of late, social media is also very popularly used for crowdsourcing. Crowdsourcing is the practice of gathering information, data, ideas and even funds as a community towards a common goal.

HOW TO CREATE A SOCIAL MEDIA MARKETING PLAN

Without a shadow of a doubt, we all know how crucial social media marketing is in today's world. Things keep changing and evolving- without using new media tools that come into our lives to innovate, upgrade, update and stay relevant.

Before you embark on social media marketing, a little bit of investment in research and a plan is always a good idea. Here are the most relevant steps you need to do when creating that perfect social media marketing campaign.

1- Start with A Reason

Your plans should start with listing out your reasons for having social media accounts. What is it that you want to achieve? What are your targets? Who is your audience? Where do they hang out? Do they even use social media? What do you want to say to them? With your team, brainstorm your reasons- if you do not already have some. Your current business plans using conventional or traditional marketing tools would already give you a good sense of what you are trying to achieve. From there on, write down your reasons and connect them with your targets and goals.

2- Develop your objectives & goals

SMM can help with a variety of marketing goals such as:

- Growing your website traffic
- Building conversions across different interest groups
- Increasing brand awareness

- Creating strong brand characteristics & personality and positive brand relationship

- Improving communication and relations with major audiences and influencers

Only when you establish your goals will you be able to achieve and measure your ROI for social media.

To make sure you stay aligned to your goals when establishing your social media marketing across different types of networks, here are some essential tips for you to remember:

- *Planning – Do a keyword search and brainstorm ideas that will attract and engage your targeted audience.*

- *Content— Consistent content reigns supreme when it comes to SMM. Ensure that you offer valuable information that your audience will find interesting to the point where they want to share, like, link or comment on your posts. Use images, videos, quotes, infographics and even GIFs to compliment your text-based content.*

- *Consistent- While each platform has its own unique audience, environment, and voice. Use these differences to tailor your messages, but always keeping in mind that your messages need to be consistent across all platforms.*

- *Blog- Having a blog and a website enables you to share a wide variety of content. Blogs are relatively easier to maintain and makes sharing information a lot faster. Your company blog is part of your social media marketing campaign because any recent social media efforts, activities, events and promos will be highlighted in your blog.*

- *Links- It isn't social media marketing if there's not sharing your unique, original content to reach out to your current followers and gaining new ones. Linking content from other parties and organizations is also part of SMM.*

- *Tracking Competitors- Tracing your competitor's activities can give you valuable insight into keyword research and other social marketing media stats. If your competitors are using a social media and you aren't doing any of it, then it's something that you get going on as well- just do it better!*

- *Analytics- What would social media marketing or traditional marketing for that matter be, if it weren't giving your some form of data? The successes of your campaigns are determined by the data you get. Google Analytics, Facebook, Instagram and Twitter Insights all have analytics that helps you measure and track your social media input so you would be able to monitor them.*

Conduct an audit on your social media

You need to assess your current situation with your social media use and how it's been working out for your so far. It is always good to go back to the drawing block and to revise, change and mix things up with your social media because after all, things change quickly. What campaigns worked for your before may not work so well now.

Conducting a social media audit includes determining who is currently connecting with you on social media, which sites your primary target market uses mainly and how your presence as a brand on social media differs from that of your competitors. HootSuite has created a [social media audit template](#) that you can use to process this information.

Social Media Audit Template

This template is to help you conduct a social media audit for your business. Follow these steps to execute your next social media audit.

Step 1
Create a spreadsheet and write down all the social networks you own and the owner for each.

Social Network	URL To Profile	Owner

Step 2
Go on Google and search up any other social media profiles that is representing your company that you don't own (imposters). Create a separate spreadsheet.

Social Network	URL	Owner	Shutdown Y/N

Step 3
Evaluate the needs for all your social media profiles and create a mission statement for each. For example: Instagram Profile—To share company culture and company achievements.

Social Network	URL to Profile	Owner	Mission Statement

SOCIAL MEDIA AUDIT TEMPLATE

Step 4
Make sure all your accounts are on brand. Proper profile photo, cover photo, icons, bios and descriptions are proper, and URL is correct.

Social Network	URL to Profile	Owner	Mission Statement	Branding Check Y/N

Step 5
Centralize the ownership of passwords.
For example: have your IT department own the key to all the passwords for the social media profiles. Use a tool like LastPass to share access on a need to use basis.

Social Network	URL to Profile	Owner	Mission Statement	Branding Check Y/N	Password Centralized Y/N

Step 6
Create a process for how new channels will be established going forward and create a criteria. Make sure to also take note of who is going to approve the requests.

For example:

- Requester:
- Who is the target audience?
- What type of content will be posted in this profile?
- Who is going to respond to content?

> Now that you've conducted your social media audit. Start managing your social media profiles with Hootsuite Pro. Sign up for a 30-day Trial of Hootsuite Pro today!

Hootsuite   SOCIAL MEDIA AUDIT TEMPLATE

This audit will give you a clearer picture of what each social account represents for your business, who is running it and what each platform's purpose is. This inventory should be updated regularly as your business grows.

You'll also want to create a mission statement for each platform. Keep them one-sentenced declarations, so there is focus on a specific goal. If you do not have a purpose for a platform, then you probably should delete it.

Here are a few mission statement examples:

Instagram: We will showcase how-to videos of how we decorate our cupcakes and connect with other fans of baking

Facebook: We will use Facebook to promote our specialty cake baking products and ingredients as well as preview videos, events that we have been invited too and events that we are organizing

Youtube: We will post our full-length video of cupcake baking tutorials

Blog: Most detailed explanations of our cupcake baking tutorials, events that we have been invited too and events that we are organizing

3- Know Your Platform

In the previous chapter, you were given a deeper understanding of each social media platform and how to sign up or open a page or account. In this section, we will give you a brief overview of how each social media platform can be used for marketing purposes, deriving full benefits from each of its unique environment.

Platform	WHAT	WHY
Facebook	Facebook is obviously one of the best social media networks for brands because of it the first one that companies joined. Companies can quickly update their page, share photos, and content with their audience. Paid advertisement is also successful on Facebook.	Every type of brand can benefit immensely from using a Facebook page. Simple to update has an ad platform and has a large audience base

	Facebook is used as a primary login for many other social apps.	
Twitter	With only 140 characters to publicize a message, brands can interact with their audience in real-time. Organic reach is always the best because all of your brand's followers will be able to view your Tweet in their feed.	Your audience wants to be able to communicate to a real person, nevermind if it's on mobile or PC. This is what makes Twitter popular. People will praise your brand and interact with your Twitter handle before anything else.
Instagram	The photo-centric and video-centric platform that makes uploading videos and photos easy. While there are paid ads, organic reach works best as people will follow what they like and want to see continuously.	Using pictures and videos to promote your brand personality is what makes Instagram a worthy social app to have. Cultivating a brand personality, giving it a humanized look and feel is what Instagram is all about. Not savvy

		for text-based promotions.
LinkedIn	It is a necessary platform for any brand- corporate or non-corporate. It is the most professional route because it is a place where brand to brand interaction takes place.	Perfect for more professional brands looking to establish themselves as serious competitors and interact with a more professional base
Pinterest	Extremely visual so if your brand is visually heavy, then Pinterest is a must. Pinterest also has promoted pins which are an avenue for advertising your brand. Pinterest is a very easy way to feature your products and curate your boards	If your brand is in the travel, fashion, food, fitness or DIY brand, Pinterest is for you. Take note that is has a vast female audience that you would need to cater to.
YouTube	It is all about video content. YouTube is the place if you want to host videos	Youtube gives the opportunity for brands to reach out to their

	whether it is DIY projects, How-Tos, and branded commercials. Vlogging, the video equivalent of blogging is an excellent way to get your brand out there.	audience via videos on all devices, at all times. People who watch video content has a higher chance of purchasing your products and services.

4- Using location-Based Social Media Tools

Networks such as Yelp, FourSquare, and Level Up are ideal for brick and mortar businesses especially car service centers, food outlets, and saloons. Use these sites to lay claim to your location spot and then increase your presence by adding in extra incentives such as check-in rewards or exclusive discounts. Be mindful of how you present your business and provide service because before you can say 'Thank you for coming' you might find a bad review on these platforms which could hurt your business.

5- Create an Editorial Calendar and Content Plan

An editorial calendar will help your structure your social media marketing plan, and this calendar should include your strategies for content creation as well as content curation. Here's a good example of social media calendar that you can use. Your marketing plan should address these elements:

- The type of content you want to post and promote
- The frequency of postings
- The target audience for each type of content
- The person in charge of content creation for the different platforms

- The promotion of content

Your calendar should also include the dates and times that you want to publish posts on your blog, photos on your Instagram and links on your Facebook or tweets to your Twitter. These kinds of things related to your very own account should be scheduled in advance, but you also need to make room for anything that happens in the world such as catastrophes and viral moments. Sometimes, you would also need to halt your social media activity in respect of a world event such as the shootings in Paris, the King of Thailand's demise and so on. You will also want to be on board with news events such as the Oscars or Emmy Awards just to keep in trend. Be spontaneous with your content, engagement and customer service.

CONCLUSION

Thank for making it through to the end of *Tractions.* Let's hope it was informative and able to provide you with all of the tools you need to achieve your goals of building your businesses traction.

The world of Social Media is a constantly evolving

one. As the years go by, newer trends are introduced, and competition gets stronger between different platforms, each one vying for the attention of the internet savvy Gen-X, Millenials and Gen-Z. Competition is good though because it brings about new features to stay relevant to its audiences, giving them better tools to share their content, better ways to engage and more interesting ways to publish content.

One of the best ways to engage in social media marketing for your business is first to use it as a personal platform for personal use. Use it as an experiment, play around with it, upload images and get used to it before you embark on opening up an account for your business. This way, you'll be better equipped to make a decision whether that particular social media is worth your time and effort or not and you will also know how audiences in different platforms react to content.

Social Media Marketing, on the other hand, has many benefits, and it does a lot to improve site traffic and help a business reach more customers. Not only that, social media marketing helps brands have a better understanding of their audience and learning from them- their purchasing habits, their likes, dislikes, interests and so on.

Any business stands a chance to lose out on its customer base if they do not evolve with current times. That said no business would lose out by investing in social media.

The next step is to start using the marketing techniques found within this book. You will be amazed at how quickly your business will start to take off.

About The Author

Hi there it's Jonathan Walker here, I want to share a little bit about myself so that we can get to know each other on a deeper level. I grew up in California, USA, and have lived there for the better part of my life. Being exposed to many different people and opportunities when I was young, it made me want to strive to become an entrepreneur to escape the rat race path that most of my peers had taken. I knew I wanted to be able to travel and experience the world the way it was meant to be seen and I've done just that. I've travelled to most places around the world and I'm enjoying every minute of it for sure. In my free time I love to play tennis and believe it or not, compose songs. I wish you all the best again in your endeavours, and may your dreams, whatever they may be, come true abundantly in the near future.

www.ingramcontent.com/pod-product-compliance
Lightning Source LLC
LaVergne TN
LVHW010331070526
838199LV00065B/5726